Introduction to Language Development